Romancing Me:
A GUIDE FOR MY MAN

Marianne Pelletier, CTR

Wally the Wellwisher Press

Romancing Me: A Guide for My Man
Marianne Pelletier, CTR

Copyright 2012 Marianne M. Pelletier

Wally the Wellwisher Press

ISBN-13: 978-0615583099
ISBN-10: 0615583091

Design and Artwork by Lighthouse24
Front Cover Photos by Yuri Arcurs/Bigstock
Back Cover Photo by Rashevskyi Viacheslav

Contents

Introduction	1
How to Use this Guide	3
About Me	**5**
In a Nutshell	7
Values	8
Desires	9
Image	10
Tastes	11
Routines	16
What I Want in a Man	20
Us When We Communicate	**21**
Us In Public	**27**
What You Do That I Adore	**33**
Us At Home	**37**
Us When We Eat	**41**
Us Apart	**47**
Us and Gifts	**51**
Us and Sex	**57**
Wrap-Up	**63**
About the Author	67

Introduction

In my tarot practice, many men ask me when they can act on their feelings for a woman, and many women ask me when their man will act. People pay me to tell them about someone else's heart: it is so unsettling to ask a person directly how he feels about you.

I wrote this workbook, *A Guide for My Man*, to help you talk to the man in your life about your needs. The companion workbook, *Romancing Me: A Guide for My Girl*, is to help your man express himself to you.

How to Use this Guide

You don't have to answer all of the questions, or look at all the sections. Use the Guide to communicate with your man.

If any part doesn't make sense to you, then skip it (if you have suggestions, though, let me know at Marianne@tarotbymarianne.com). Add your own notes anywhere you feel like, especially if one of your choices is a surprise to your man.

Please use this book to open conversation, explore each other's needs, and say things that you have had trouble saying aloud. You may find that you'd like to try a little bit of leather in the bedroom, or breakfast in bed, or a risqué smooch in public. Wouldn't it be wonderful if he's delighted by the idea?

 # *About Me*

– *In a Nutshell* –

I am:
- ❏ Visual – I love to look at things
- ❏ Auditory – I'm into the sound of things
- ❏ Tactile – I like what I can touch

My favorite color is: _____

My favorite sound is: _____
_____

My favorite fabric or sensation is: _____
_____

I am:
- ❏ Spontaneous
- ❏ Planful
- ❏ Laid back
- ❏ Control freaky
- ❏ Playful
- ❏ Quiet/peaceful
- ❏ Committed/focused
- ❏ Quick
- ❏ A born again Christian
- ❏ I describe myself this way: _____
_____

- In a Nutshell - (continued)

My astrological sign is:
- ❏ Not important to me
- ❏ Aries
- ❏ Taurus
- ❏ Gemini
- ❏ Cancer
- ❏ Leo
- ❏ Virgo
- ❏ Libra
- ❏ Scorpio
- ❏ Sagittarius
- ❏ Capricorn
- ❏ Aquarius
- ❏ Pisces

– Values –

What I value most is:
- ❏ Wealth
- ❏ Love
- ❏ Fame
- ❏ Beauty
- ❏ Intelligence
- ❏ Accomplishment
- ❏ Courage
- ❏ Respect
- ❏ Family
- ❏ My career
- ❏ Fun
- ❏ Extravagance

(list continues . . .)

- Values - (continued)

- ❏ Frugality
- ❏ Intellect
- ❏ Justice
- ❏ Joy/happiness
- ❏ Open mindedness
- ❏ Tradition
- ❏ Opulence
- ❏ Fresh air
- ❏ Excitement
- ❏ Sex
- ❏ My religious or spiritual practice
- ❏ Something else: _____

– Desires –

What I want most from a relationship is:

- ❏ Validation
- ❏ Respect
- ❏ Love
- ❏ Family
  - ❏ Including children
- ❏ Fun
- ❏ Companionship
- ❏ Pride
- ❏ Sex
- ❏ Something else: _____

– Image –

I want to be seen as:
- ❏ Gorgeous
- ❏ A Princess
- ❏ The center of your universe
- ❏ Sexy
- ❏ Luscious
- ❏ Fair
- ❏ Adorable
- ❏ Powerful
- ❏ Wise
- ❏ Strong
- ❏ Exciting
- ❏ Rich
- ❏ Brave
- ❏ Funny
- ❏ Loving
- ❏ Dependable
- ❏ Safe
- ❏ Supportive
- ❏ Athletic
- ❏ This: _____

_____

When I dress, it's for:
- ❏ Comfort
- ❏ Style
- ❏ Function
- ❏ Showing off my delectable body
- ❏ Expression of my femininity
- ❏ To look better than other women

(list continues . . .)

- *Image* - *(continued)*

- ❏ Expression of my power/wealth
- ❏ Expression of my creativity/color
- ❏ Expression of my interests
- ❏ This: _____

_____

– *Tastes* –

I have a:
- ❏ Sweet tooth
- ❏ Salt tooth
- ❏ Focus on healthy eating
- ❏ Taste that runs this way: _____

_____

Around alcohol, I:
- ❏ Do not drink alcohol
- ❏ Am a wine drinker
- ❏ Am a beer drinker
- ❏ Am a liquor drinker
- ❏ Am a mixed drink fan, especially: ___

_____

- ❏ Drink mostly: _____
- ❏ I only drink when: _____

For entertainment, I:
- ❏ Shop!
- ❏ Hang out with my friends

(list continues . . .)

- Tastes - (continued)

- ❏ Talk to people on the phone
- ❏ Enjoy the theater
- ❏ Would be really making a sacrifice to go to a play or musical
- ❏ Like museums
- ❏ Would rather not go to museums
- ❏ Like opera
- ❏ Like concerts
- ❏ Go to a special place

Please don't ever make me go to: _____

I would really be delighted to get tickets for: ___

When it comes to sports, I:
- ❏ Play sports
- ❏ Watch sports
- ❏ Love to watch my man play sports
- ❏ Love to tailgate
- ❏ Play sports on my gadget: _____

- ❏ Have a fantasy sports team: _____

- ❏ Will not keep you company while you play sports on your gadget or fiddle with your fantasy sports team
- ❏ Can take or leave sports
- ❏ Hate sports

(list continues . . .)

- Tastes - (continued)

❏ My favorite sport to play: _____

_____

❏ My favorite sport to watch: _____

_____

❏ My favorite sport to watch you play:

_____

❏ My favorite team: _____

_____

I also:
- ❏ Dig music
- ❏ Don't dig music much
- ❏ Use music as a background

My favorite style is:
- ❏ Rock
- ❏ Rap
- ❏ Symphonic
- ❏ Jazz
- ❏ Country
- ❏ Christian
- ❏ Hip-hop
- ❏ Softer stuff
- ❏ Folk
- ❏ Bluegrass
- ❏ Dance
- ❏ This: _____

My favorite artist is: _____

_____

- Tastes - (continued)

I:

❏ Play an instrument: _____
❏ Play an air: _____

❏ I don't dance
❏ I like to dance:
    ❏ Ballroom
    ❏ Waltz
    ❏ Rumba
    ❏ Tango
    ❏ Folk
    ❏ Swing
    ❏ Disco
    ❏ Hip-hop
    ❏ Punk
    ❏ Slow and romantic
    ❏ Line dancing
    ❏ Two-step
    ❏ Contra

❏ I like movies:
    ❏ At home
    ❏ At the theatre
    ❏ On my gadget: _____
    ❏ My favorite movie genre is:_____

    _____

    ❏ My favorite movie is:_____

    _____

- Tastes - (continued)

- ❏ I like the outdoors:
    - ❏ At the mountains
    - ❏ At the ocean
    - ❏ In the woods
    - ❏ On a lake
    - ❏ Camping
    - ❏ Wherever you want as long as you plan it and drive
    - ❏ Yard sales or driving
    - ❏ Picnics
    - ❏ This: _____
    - ❏ My favorite outdoor activity is: _____
    _____

- ❏ I prefer indoors:
    - ❏ At the mall/outlets
    - ❏ At the spa
    - ❏ At home
    - ❏ Here: _____

Politically, I lean:
- ❏ Left   ❏ Center   ❏ Right
- ❏ Feminist   ❏ Old fashioned girl
- ❏ Centrist   ❏ Unique
- ❏ Like this: _____

. . . and I am:
- ❏ Not interested in politics
- ❏ Registered as | ❏ Akin to
    - ❏ Democrats
    - ❏ Republicans
    - ❏ Independents
    - ❏ This party: _____

(list continues . . .)

- Tastes - (continued)

❏ Working hard at empowering girls and women
❏ Helping children become good citizens
❏ Interested in a peaceful world

❏ I volunteer with: _____

❏ I wish I could help with: _____

❏ I'm very active with this organization: _____

For religion, I practice:
  ❏ Christianity
  ❏ Judaism
  ❏ Buddhism
  ❏ Wiccan
  ❏ This: _____
  ❏ I'm spiritual more than religious
  ❏ I don't believe in that stuff

– Routines –

I have the most energy in the:
  ❏ Morning
  ❏ Afternoon
  ❏ Evening
  ❏ Nighttime

Right after work I:
  ❏ Take off my work clothes and get comfortable
  (list continues . . .)

- Routines - (continued)

- ❏ Call a friend
- ❏ Call my special man
- ❏ Get a drink at my favorite bar
- ❏ Go to the gym
- ❏ Blast the radio
- ❏ Nap
- ❏ Eat
- ❏ Veg out in front of the TV
- ❏ This: _____

These are my hobbies:
- ❏ Dancing to: _____
- ❏ Karaoke
- ❏ Cooking: _____
- ❏ Cards/Magic/Dungeons: _____
  _____
- ❏ Gaming:
    - ❏ Gambling
    - ❏ Fantasy/role playing
    - ❏ Other: _____
- ❏ Reading, especially: _____
  _____
- ❏ Gardening:
    - ❏ Flowers
    - ❏ Food
    - ❏ This: _____
- ❏ Cars:
    - ❏ Driving
    - ❏ Fixing
    - ❏ Looking at
    - ❏ My favorite car: _____

(list continues . . .)

- Routines - (continued)

- ❏ Horses
- ❏ Motorcycles
- ❏ Running/jogging/biking
- ❏ Swimming/water sports
- ❏ Yoga
- ❏ Getting a massage
    - ❏ At the spa
    - ❏ I have a personal therapist
    - ❏ From you
- ❏ Photography:
    - ❏ Digital
    - ❏ Film
    - ❏ I like to photograph: _____
- ❏ Collecting: _____
- ❏ Backpacking:
    - ❏ Into the woods
    - ❏ Up mountains
    - ❏ Rock climbing
    - ❏ Here: _____
- ❏ Fishing:
    - ❏ Fly
    - ❏ Spin
- ❏ Geocoaching
- ❏ Leather working
- ❏ Bowling:
    - ❏ Competitively
    - ❏ League
    - ❏ For fun
- ❏ Martial arts: _____
- ❏ Wine/beer/whiskey/scotch tasting
- ❏ Gourmet food

(list continues . . .)

- Routines - (continued)

- ❏ Flying/parachuting/hang gliding
- ❏ Debating/politics
- ❏ Blogging/writing
- ❏ Drawing/Painting
- ❏ Paintball
- ❏ Brewing beer or wine
- ❏ Canning/preserving
- ❏ Working on my house
- ❏ Painting
- ❏ Renaissance fairs or period play acting
- ❏ Antiquing
- ❏ Decorating
- ❏ This: _____

_____
_____

– What I Want in a Man –

The kind of man I fall in love with has these traits:
- ❏ Strong
- ❏ Romantic
- ❏ Passionate
- ❏ Loving
- ❏ Patient
- ❏ Gentle
- ❏ Rich
- ❏ Powerful
- ❏ Ordinary guy
- ❏ Generous
- ❏ A leader
- ❏ Handsome
- ❏ Fun
- ❏ Athletic
- ❏ This: _____

Us When We Communicate

– *Communication* –

More often than not, I prefer that we make our plans through:
- ❏ Phone calls
- ❏ Text messages
- ❏ I.M.
- ❏ E-mail
- ❏ In person

…and I usually like to do this:
- ❏ On the spot
- ❏ Ahead of time
- ❏ Depends on the plan

When we communicate, please be:
- ❏ Frank
- ❏ Gentle
- ❏ Open to humor
- ❏ Affectionate
- ❏ A good listener
- ❏ Encouraging
- ❏ This: _____

Frankly, I'd rather that
- ❏ I make:
    - ❏ Most
    - ❏ All of the plans:
        - ❏ So I can surprise you
        - ❏ Because I'm a control freak

(list continues . . .)

- *Communication* - *(continued)*

- ❏ You make:
  - ❏ Most
  - ❏ All of the plans:
    - ❏ Because you come up with really good ideas
    - ❏ Because you're a control freak
    - ❏ Because I don't really care what we do or where we go

Love notes are:
- ❏ Fantastic and I love getting them:
  - ❏ When I get home
  - ❏ In my bag
  - ❏ Somewhere surprising
- ❏ Not really my favorites

If you write me love notes, please make them:
- ❏ Sentimental
- ❏ Admiring
- ❏ Erotic
- ❏ Something else: _____

_____

While we're talking, I feel most comfortable when you:
- ❏ Listen without interrupting me
- ❏ Interject your thoughts and confirmation

(list continues . . .)

- *Communication - (continued)*

- ❏ Keep eye contact
- ❏ Keep the conversation simple
- ❏ Reassure me with touches
- ❏ Bring up topics that are fun or interesting to both of us
- ❏ Something else: _____

_____

_____

 # *Us In Public*

– In Public –

When you look at me, I feel:
- ❑ Contented
- ❑ Aroused
- ❑ Joyful
- ❑ Courted
- ❑ In love
- ❑ Cute
- ❑ Gorgeous
- ❑ Adored
- ❑ This: _____

When we are out with our friends, I feel:
- ❑ Flattered
- ❑ Happier
- ❑ Like a woman
- ❑ Honored when you:
    - ❑ Dress up
    - ❑ Wear cologne
    - ❑ Put your hand on the small of my back
    - ❑ Flirt with me
    - ❑ Say my name with your special voice
    - ❑ Show off how smart you are
    - ❑ Show off how smart I am
    - ❑ Listen to my stories even though you've heard them

(list continues . . .)

- In Public - (continued)

- ❏ Make me laugh
- ❏ Pose for me and others with that gorgeous body of yours
- ❏ Stand up for me
- ❏ Stand up for yourself
- ❏ Make everyone laugh
- ❏ Make everyone feel included
- ❏ Something else: _____

_____

When we're out with others, I wish you would:

- ❏ Stay near me
- ❏ Let me visit with others
- ❏ Flirt with others so they can see you going home with me
- ❏ Charm others like you charm me
- ❏ Show off your fantastic:
  - ❏ Body
  - ❏ Mind
  - ❏ Wallet
  - ❏ This: _____
- ❏ Get just as playful as I'm getting
- ❏ Demonstrate your dignity
- ❏ Take care of me
- ❏ Something else: _____

_____

I want your family to know: _____

_____

- In Public - (continued)

My favorite place for you to touch me in public is:
- ❏ My shoulder
- ❏ My back
- ❏ My arm
- ❏ My knee
- ❏ This spot: _____

_____

I:
- ❏ Love
- ❏ Am not much into:
    - ❏ You wearing cologne like:
    _____
    - ❏ You wearing a natural scent, like: _____
    - ❏ Your musky, manly scent

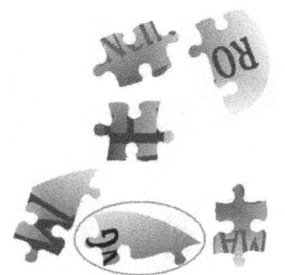
What You Do That I Adore

– What I Adore –

The outfit you wear that's my favorite is: _____

_____

You spoil me like mad when you:
- ❏ Listen
- ❏ Let me put my head on your lap
- ❏ Compliment me
- ❏ Pick up the check
- ❏ Brag about being with me
- ❏ Show a little jealousy
- ❏ Give me a backrub
- ❏ Make me a snack or meal
- ❏ Clean for me
- ❏ Seduce me
- ❏ Take care of my: _____

_____

- ❏ Something else: _____

_____

The most sexually attractive part of you is your:

_____

The thing you do that is the biggest turn on for me is: _____

_____

- *What I Adore* - *(continued)*

I love it most when you:

- ❏ Suggest my favorite restaurant for our dates
- ❏ Offer to stay home instead of going out
- ❏ Buy me tickets to that performance I love
- ❏ Watch my favorite movie with me
- ❏ Bring over my favorite food/drink
- ❏ Brag about me on your social network page
- ❏ Challenge my mind
- ❏ Beat me at _____
- ❏ Share your day or your feelings
- ❏ Walk up to me and start ripping our clothes off
- ❏ This: _____

_____
_____
_____

# Us At Home

– At Home –

The way I'd want you to wake me is:
- ❏ Please don't, you know how grumpy I am
- ❏ Bring coffee
- ❏ Kiss me
- ❏ Bring food: _____

When we are having a quiet evening or day at home, I'd really rather:
- ❏ Sit around like a slug
- ❏ Cuddle
- ❏ Watch my favorite TV: _____
  _____
- ❏ Play a:
  - ❏ Video game
    - ❏ With you
    - ❏ By myself
  - ❏ Board game
  - ❏ Card game
- ❏ Stay in bed:
  - ❏ Until we're both in the mood to make love
  - ❏ Until we're both too hungry to stay
  - ❏ Until it's time for my favorite TV
  - ❏ Until: _____
  _____

(list continues . . .)

- At Home - (continued)

- ❏ Sit and read:
    - ❏ To you
    - ❏ With you
    - ❏ Next to you
- ❏ Snuggle with our laptops, iPads, or iPhones and keep each other company

I also:

- ❏ Like pets
- ❏ Have a pet
- ❏ Am not into pets
- ❏ Something else: _____

_____

I:

- ❏ Am into bubble baths
- ❏ Take long, hot baths
- ❏ Sing in the shower
- ❏ Take quick showers – it's just to get clean
- ❏ Love to shower with my man

# *Us When We Eat*

– *When We Eat* –

Around food and romance, I prefer:
- ❏ Eating out:
  - ❏ The cuisine doesn't matter:
    - ❏ As long as the food is good
    - ❏ As long as the restaurant is fancy
    - ❏ As long as I'm seen with you
    - ❏ As long as you like it
    - ❏ As long as the meals are
      - ❏ Generous
      - ❏ Healthy
  - ❏ For restaurants, I really like:
    - ❏ Sports bars/pub food
    - ❏ Steak houses/chop shops
    - ❏ Hamburgers
    - ❏ Pizza
    - ❏ Wings
    - ❏ Sandwich shops
    - ❏ Diners
    - ❏ Ethnic or international: _
      _____
    - ❏ Family restaurants
    - ❏ Healthy
    - ❏ Vegetarian
    - ❏ Vegan

    (list continues . . .)

- When We Eat - (continued)

- ❑ Something nearby
- ❑ Someplace hard to get a reservation for
- ❑ Someplace quiet and intimate
- ❑ Elegant
- ❑ Bistros
- ❑ Upscale
- ❑ My own style: _____
  _____

❑ Eating at home, and:
- ❑ I cook
- ❑ You cook

❑ Eating at home and ordering in:
- ❑ Pizza
- ❑ Sandwiches
- ❑ Chinese
- ❑ Italian
- ❑ Mexican
- ❑ Something else: _____
  _____

My favorite meal that you:
- ❑ Make
- ❑ Buy
- ❑ Eat that I make

  is: _____

This is my favorite dessert: _____

- When We Eat - (continued)

When I'm eating, I really prefer:
- ❏ Formal dining – even at home I like linen on the table.
- ❏ Casual dining
- ❏ Totally casual dining –just hand me my plate and then move so I can watch TV
- ❏ Adventurous dining, including picnics or mystery theatre
- ❏ Other: _____

Us Apart

– *Apart* –

- ❑ I like to carry a memento of us with me when I'm away from you:
    - ❑ A lock of your hair
    - ❑ The last t-shirt you wore
    - ❑ The last note you wrote me
    - ❑ A photo of us
    - ❑ A photo of you
    - ❑ Something else:_____
- ❑ Instead, I think of memories of our time together as the best mementos

When we're apart for a period of time, I like to:
- ❑ Have a phone call with you at a set time
- ❑ Send you surprise texts or e-mails from time to time
- ❑ Think fondly of you while I concentrate on what I'm away for

When I'm not with my man, I tend to:
- ❑ Focus on the job at hand
- ❑ Buy little presents for my love
- ❑ Like to know where you are and what you're up to
- ❑ Work hard at getting back to you
- ❑ Hang out with my friends to have a balanced life
- ❑ Call you often to hear your voice

 # *Us and Gifts*

– *Gifts* –

I prefer goods:
- ❏ Jewelry
- ❏ Scents
- ❏ Food
- ❏ Games/electronics
- ❏ Things for my house:_____
_____

- ❏ Clothing
- ❏ Books
- ❏ You in a red ribbon
- ❏ Something for my hobby:
- ❏ Tickets to: _____
_____

- ❏ Gift cards for:_____
_____

- ❏ A pet:_____
- ❏ A trip to:_____
_____

- ❏ Sporting goods like:_____
_____

About flowers – I:
- ❏ Like flowers
- ❏ Am not much into flowers

(list continues . . .)

- Gifts - (continued)

❏ My favorite flowers are: _____
_____

❏ You can send me flowers at work
❏ Please send me flowers only at home
❏ You can send me flowers even though I live with my parents
❏ Please don't send me flowers
    ❏ But you can bring some
    ❏ And don't bring any, either

I prefer services:
❏ A massage:
    ❏ That you do
    ❏ That you buy me
❏ Buy me a:
    ❏ Personal trainer
    ❏ Coach to have a better _____
    _____ game
❏ Day at the:
    ❏ Spa
    ❏ Circus
    ❏ Beach
    ❏ Ski slope
    ❏ Zoo
    ❏ Shopping: _____
_____

(list continues . . .)

- Gifts - (continued)

- ❑ Races
    - ❑ Horse
    - ❑ Dog
    - ❑ Car: _____
    - ❑ Bicycle
    - ❑ People: _____
    - ❑ Extreme: _____
    - ❑ Triathlon
    - ❑ Boats: _____
    - ❑ Something else: _____

_____

- ❑ Game/match _____
- ❑ Fair/festival: _____
- ❑ Museum: _____
- ❑ Farm/ranch:_____
- ❑ Park:
    - ❑ Amusement
    - ❑ State
    - ❑ Bike/skateboard
    - ❑ Snowboard
- ❑ Range:
    - ❑ Shooting
    - ❑ Archery
    - ❑ This: _____

_____

(list continues . . .)

- Gifts - (continued)

- ❏ Clean my:
    - ❏ House
    - ❏ Garage
    - ❏ Car
    - ❏ Office
    - ❏ Something else: _____
- ❏ Give me a free night out with my friends:
    - ❏ Every once in awhile
    - ❏ Often

I prefer clothing:

- ❏ Please don't buy me clothes; I'm better at buying my own
- ❏ Oh, honey, just buy me jewelry
- ❏ I love receiving these kinds of clothing from my man:
    - ❏ Hats
    - ❏ Dresses:
        - ❏ Formal
        - ❏ Cocktail
        - ❏ Casual
    - ❏ Lingerie:
        - ❏ Feel free to buy me something spicy for under there
        - ❏ Whatever makes your eyes light up when I wear it
        - ❏ Something comfy

 # *Us and Sex*

– *Sex* –

- [ ] Sexually, I am:
    - [ ] Romantic
    - [ ] Hot and fast
    - [ ] Playful
    - [ ] Teasing
    - [ ] Rough

What sex means to me is that it:
- [ ] Shares love with you
- [ ] Shows you and me how beautiful we are
- [ ] Offers a playful way to be intimate
- [ ] Shares our love of God or our Creator
- [ ] Celebrates our relationship
- [ ] Relieves stress
- [ ] Makes me feel beautiful or good looking
- [ ] Something else: _____

_____

About BDSM, I:
- [ ] Don't know what that is
- [ ] Have experimented
- [ ] Like the idea
- [ ] Have a dungeon in my house

. . . and I am:
- [ ] A Top

(list continues . . .)

- Sex - (continued)

- ❏ A Bottom
- ❏ I don't know what this is

I like to have sex:
- ❏ At home where it's private
- ❏ In places where we might get caught
- ❏ Out in nature
- ❏ All over the house
- ❏ In water
- ❏ In my vehicle
- ❏ In your vehicle
- ❏ On the phone
- ❏ Online
- ❏ Here: _____

Here is my one favorite position: _____

_____

Here is the one thing I've wanted to try with you and haven't mentioned it yet: _____

_____

_____

The longest time I've had sex continuously was:
- ❏ Counted in hours
- ❏ Counted in days
- ❏ It's not the time, it's the quality that counts

- Sex - (continued)

During sex, I like to add:
- ❏ Food that we can play with
- ❏ Gels or lotions
- ❏ Tantalizing clothing: _____
  _____

- ❏ Role playing
- ❏ Soft fabrics
- ❏ Rough fabrics and items
- ❏ Dirty language
- ❏ Erotic but sweet language
- ❏ Music
- ❏ Ice
- ❏ Candle wax
- ❏ Blindfolds
- ❏ Handcuffs or other binding equipment
- ❏ Another person: _____
  _____

- ❏ Video/Photographs
- ❏ Pornography
- ❏ Something else: _____
  _____

Here is one more thing I want to tell you about our lovemaking: _____
_____
_____

Wrap-up: Tell Him How You Feel

This page is for you to share anything at all with your man. If you're stuck for words, just name the song that would do it for you. Well done!

About the Author

Marianne Pelletier is a certified tarot reader and practicing psychic. Marianne's writing on romance and flirting, and personal journeys appear in various formats, from small poetry magazines to Helium.com and triond.com.

She lives in Upstate New York with her partner, Laura.

www.ingramcontent.com/pod-product-compliance
Lightning Source LLC
Chambersburg PA
CBHW071750040426
42446CB00012B/2510